Protocol Development and Biological and Physical Characterization of Streams in Wrangell-St. Elias National Park and Preserve

Results of the 2006 Central Alaska Network flowing waters pilot study

Natural Resource Technical Report NPS/CAKN/NRTR—2009/217

Trey Simmons
National Park Service
4175 Geist Road
Fairbanks, Alaska 99709

May 2009

U.S. Department of the Interior
National Park Service
Natural Resource Program Center
Fort Collins, Colorado

The Natural Resource Publication series addresses natural resource topics that are of interest and applicability to a broad readership in the National Park Service and to others in the management of natural resources, including the scientific community, the public, and the NPS conservation and environmental constituencies. Manuscripts are peer-reviewed to ensure that the information is scientifically credible, technically accurate, appropriately written for the intended audience, and is designed and published in a professional manner.

The Natural Resource Technical Reports series is used to disseminate the peer-reviewed results of scientific studies in the physical, biological, and social sciences for both the advancement of science and the achievement of the National Park Service's mission. The reports provide contributors with a forum for displaying comprehensive data that are often deleted from journals because of page limitations. Current examples of such reports include the results of research that addresses natural resource management issues; natural resource inventory and monitoring activities; resource assessment reports; scientific literature reviews; and peer reviewed proceedings of technical workshops, conferences, or symposia.

Views, statements, findings, conclusions, recommendations and data in this report are solely those of the author(s) and do not necessarily reflect views and policies of the U.S. Department of the Interior, NPS. Mention of trade names or commercial products does not constitute endorsement or recommendation for use by the National Park Service.

This report is available from the Central Alaska Network website (http://science.nature.nps.gov/im/units/cakn/reportpubs.cfm) and the Natural Resource Publications Management website (http://www.nature.nps.gov/publications/NRPM).

NPS 100026, May 2009

Contents

Figures

Tables

Abstract

This report describes the results of the 2006 field season for the Central Alaska Network (CAKN) flowing waters monitoring program. The key objectives for the 2006 field season were to assess the logistics involved in various sampling approaches and to collect data from a variety of streams as a way to begin to determine the range of natural variability for various candidate biological, chemical and physical metrics. I was able to collect data at 13 study sites located throughout WRST. Two of these sites were visited in two different seasons (summer and autumn) to assess seasonal variability, which was substantial for invertebrates and diatoms and moderate for water chemistry parameters. At one of these sites, multiple replicate biological samples were collected to assess sampling variability. For both invertebrates and diatoms, intersample variability was small, indicating that the composite samples collected are representative of reach biodiversity, at least at this stream. Over the course of the summer, I was able to get the sampling protocols fairly well defined, although more work will be required next year to work out the kinks. Some aspects were only attempted at a few sites (*e.g.*, fish sampling was only conducted at 3 of the sites). Similarly, laboratory protocols were largely worked out and the development of operational taxonomic units for macroinvertebrates was begun. Despite the relatively small number of sites sampled, I was able to capture a surprising amount of variability in physical, chemical and biological characteristics. A total of 84 unique macroinvertebrate taxa were collected, with richness at individual sites varying from 4 to 30 unique taxa. Diatom richness was apparently much higher, with 166 unique species identified and richness at individual sites varying from 8 to 59 species. The difference may be partially attributable to the higher level of taxonomic resolution for the diatom samples.

Acknowledgements

I would like to thank Jeff Ostermiller, Sara Goeking, Alex Anderson, Dave Galbraith and Mike Knoche for assistance in the field and for multiple invaluable contributions to the development of the sampling protocol. I would also like to thank the staff of Wrangell-St. Elias National Park and Preserve, in particular Eric Veach, Dave Sarafin and Pete Dalton, for their assistance with both data collection and the planning and execution of the Chitina River expedition, and for valuable discussions about the park and the monitoring program. Finally, I'd like to thank Maggie MacCluskie for her unflagging support, intellectual, financial and moral, as I struggled through my first field season.

Introduction

This study is part of the National Park Service Vital Signs Monitoring Program for the Central Alaska Network. Climate change and other anthropogenic impacts can be expected to have a dramatic effect on CAKN freshwater ecosystems; the streams and rivers portion of the Vital Signs program will be designed to detect trends in the status of important components of lotic ecosystems. These include hydrologic regime, geomorphology, water quality and the distribution and abundance of freshwater fish, benthic macroinvertebrate and diatom species. Fundamentally, the goal is to develop a logistically feasible, repeatable and scientifically robust monitoring program. To the extent possible, we intend to incorporate indicators, data and methods developed as part of the DENA Long Term Ecological Monitoring (LTEM) program. The sampling design has not yet been finalized; however, it will include a combination of probabilistic site selection to allow park-wide estimates of average condition, and the use of fixed and readily accessible sentinel sites to increase sensitivity to temporal changes.

Like streams everywhere, the characteristics and dynamics of stream ecosystems in the Central Alaska Network are influenced at a variety of spatial and temporal scales by physical, chemical, meteorological and biological phenomena. Factors such as basin geology, topography, climate and terrestrial vegetation community are nearly universal drivers of stream ecosystem structure and dynamics. Due to the extreme climate that characterizes arctic and subarctic regions, the streams of the Central Alaska Network are substantially affected by extreme winters, glaciation and permafrost. These differences present unique challenges as well as providing an important opportunity to document the expected dramatic alterations in these systems in response to climate change. Melting permafrost can be expected to have a substantial effect on nutrient concentrations and transport, as well as on hydrologic regime and connectivity between lakes and streams within catchments. The extent of glaciation within stream and river basins has a profound influence on all aspects of lotic ecosystems. Glacially-dominated streams tend to be highly dynamic and extensively braided, with a hydrograph that is characterized by extreme diurnal fluctuations in the summer months. Ongoing climate warming can be expected to alter these systems dramatically as glacial melting accelerates, the melting season increases in length, and glaciers continue to retreat. The CAKN flowing water monitoring program will be designed to capture the effects of these and other potential changes on important aspects of stream ecosystem structure and function.

The selection of appropriate metrics is a critical step in the design of any monitoring program. Because of the size and remoteness of its component park units, CAKN presents unique challenges. Few baseline data are available for any of the potential metrics, which makes *a priori* decisions about which may be most useful problematic. The difficulty and cost of accessing remote study sites, in combination with the sheer size of CAKN will limit the density of, and return interval to, monitoring sites. This in turn constrains which metrics can be usefully included in a monitoring program. For these and other reasons, pilot studies to test data collection methods and to estimate baseline values and variances for potential metrics are critical to the future success of any monitoring program. Therefore, the major focus of this study is on the development work needed to design and implement a comprehensive and robust ecological monitoring program. All of the field work in 2006 was conducted in WRST.

1

There were two objectives for the 2006 field season. The primary objective was to begin to assess the feasibility of various data collection protocols. A major component of this effort was a float trip on the Chitina River in June, on which I was accompanied by a number of knowledgeable scientists, including both WRST staff and consulting experts.

The Chitina River float trip, though something of a disappointment from a purely data-oriented standpoint, was highly successfully in terms of protocol development. The presence of 4 experienced field biologists with whom I was comfortable greatly facilitated the rapid assembly of a set of potentially useful approaches to characterizing and sampling not only simple wadeable streams, but also braided channels and large, non-wadeable rivers. We also initiated development of a riparian vegetation characterization and sampling protocol that would generate data consistent with the data collected in the CAKN vegetation monitoring program.

The second objective was to begin to characterize the range of natural biological and physical variability among WRST streams and rivers. This included sampling benthic macroinvertebrates and diatoms, fish and riparian vegetation, and collecting detailed water chemistry and physical habitat data. To begin an assessment of spatial variability, streams were sampled in 3 different areas of the park: in the Chitina River valley, along the Nabesna Road, and in the remote northeast section. I also sampled 2 Nabesna Road sites in 2 different seasons to address questions of seasonal variability and one site multiple times during a single visit to assess sampling variability. The results of these studies are presented below.

Methods

Study Area

The sampling took place in 3 areas of Wrangell-St. Elias National Park and Preserve (WRST): in the Chitina River valley, along the Nabesna Road, and in the remote northeastern corner of the park (Figure 1). While this limited set of sites cannot adequately characterize the ecological and physical variability of WRST streams, I was able to visit 3 widely separated areas and therefore at least begin to estimate the spatial variation in key metrics. These areas also represent 4 of the major river basins that drain WRST – the Chitina River, the upper Copper River, the Nabesna River and the White River, and 4 of the 8 major ecoregions in the park (Kluane Range, Alaska Range, Wrangell Mountains and Copper River Basin).

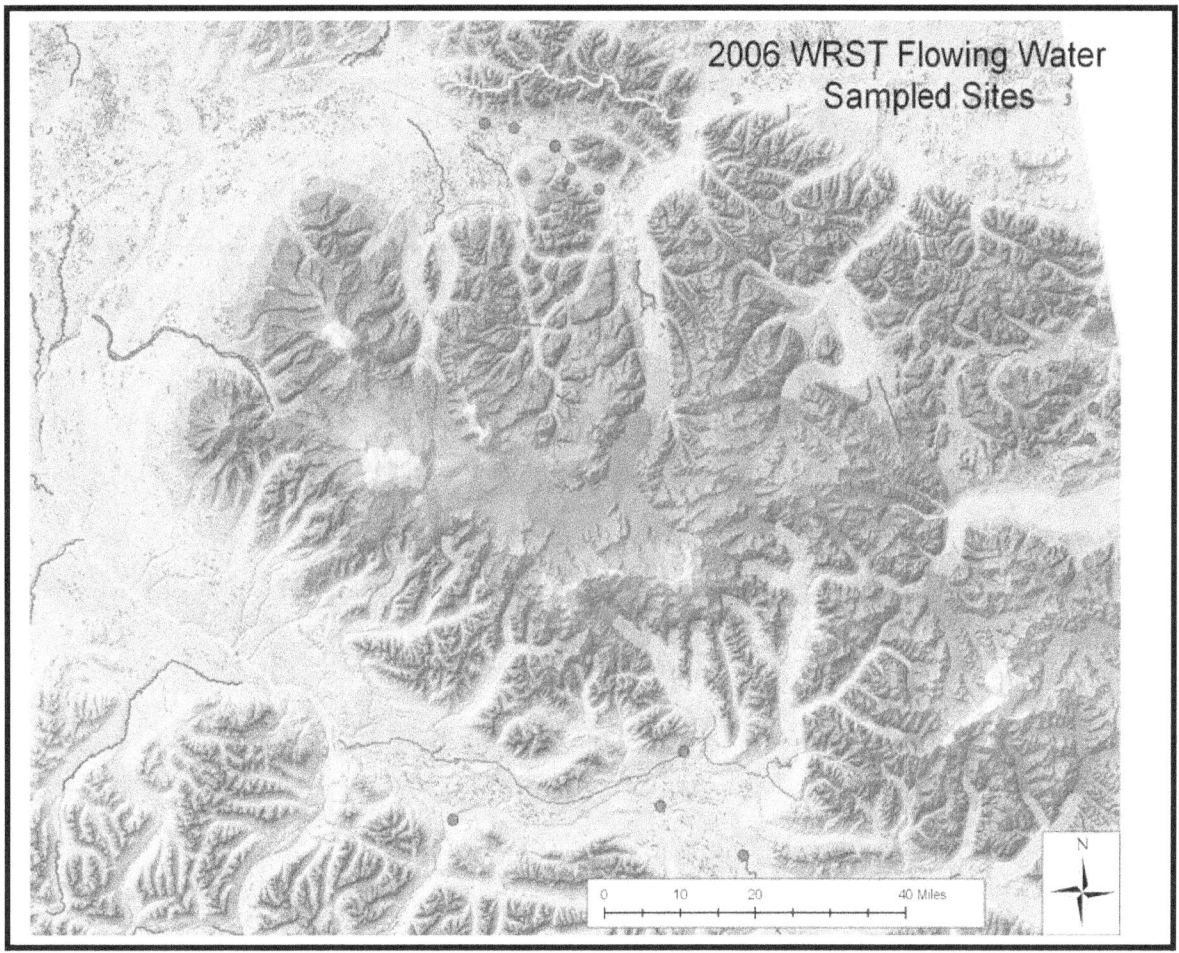

Figure 1. Locations of 2006 WRST study sites. Red dots identify sampling locations. The park boundary is shown in turquoise, the Nabesna and McCarthy roads are shown in brown.

Site Selection

Site accessibility is a substantial problem for ecological studies in most of Alaska, and WRST is no exception, despite the presence of the McCarthy and Nabesna Roads. In an attempt to minimize site access costs for the 2006 sampling season, I decided to limit my sampling universe to sites that could be accessed by road or fixed-wing aircraft; in addition, a number of tributaries to the Chitina River were selected that were to be sampled during a river trip on the Chitina River in June. A total of 97 potential sampling sites were included in the list (Figure 2). Because the primary purpose of the 2006 field season was to evaluate protocols, sites were prioritized according to convenience rather than being selected using a probabilistic design. During the course of the field season, I visited or flew over 58 of these 97 sites and evaluated them for sampling.

Of the 58 sites I evaluated, 30 (52%) were dry at the time of the sampling visit or overflight. A number of these streams were flowing when I scouted sites on the McCarthy and Nabesna Roads in May, but it is unclear whether the majority are truly seasonal or more classically intermittent (most flow during storm events). At least one site (Gravel Creek – Site 007) that was flowing at the time of sampling was later determined (through consultation with local residents) to be an intermittent stream, which is consistent with the extremely low macroinvertebrate taxa richness and abundance observed. Based on these observations, supplemented by discussions with local residents, it appears that a substantial fraction, if not a majority, of the streams that are shown as being perennial on blue-line maps of WRST (*e.g.*, USGS quads) actually have intermittent flow.

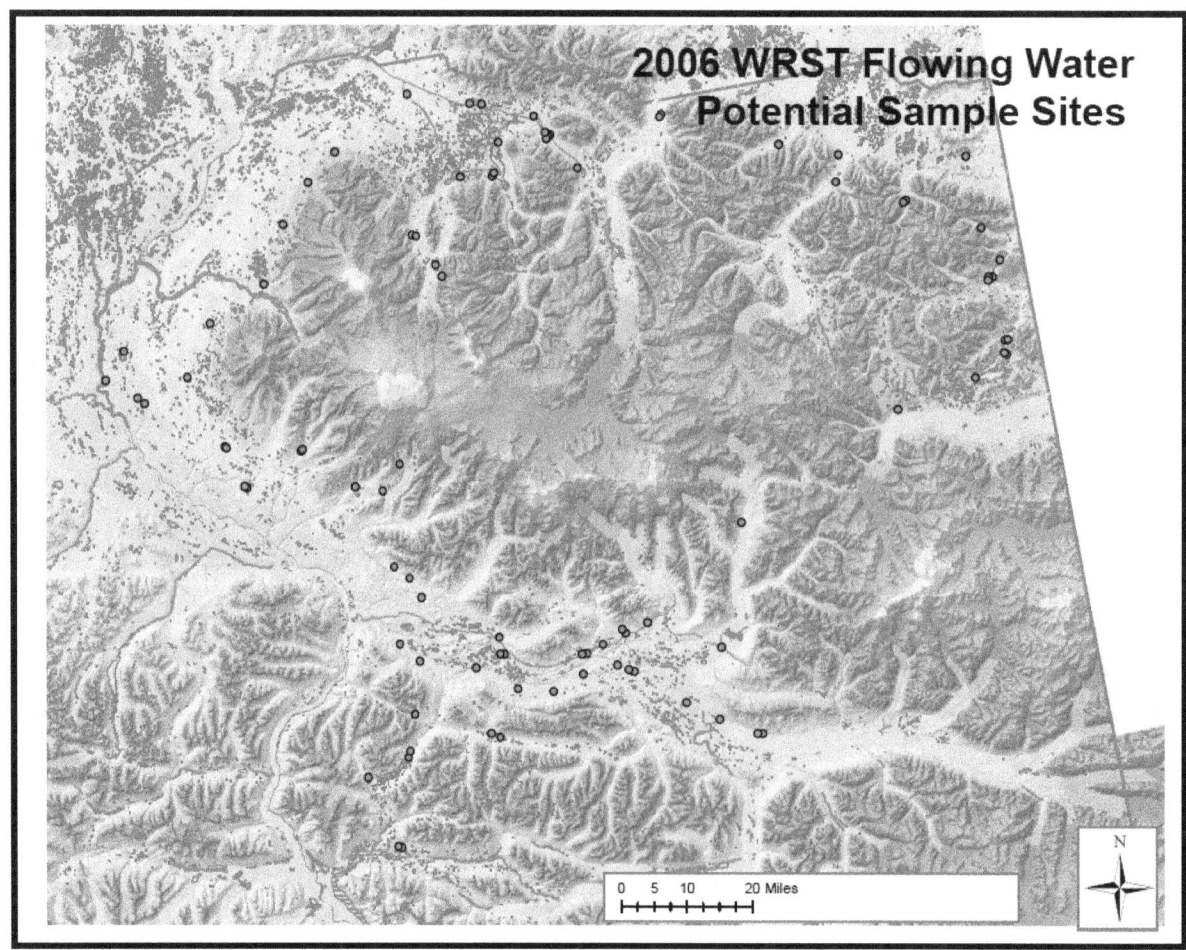

Figure 2. Locations of the 97 potential sampling locations selected for the 2006 field season.

4

An examination of the updated National Hydrography Dataset (NHD), recently released by the USGS, reveals an identical problem (100% of stream miles in WRST are identified as perennial in the NHD). This greatly complicates *a priori* selection of sampling locations, and given the high cost of accessing remote sites, presents a substantial challenge to the program.

An important, though only partial, solution will be to consult with local residents and park staff prior to the field season to determine which streams are thought to be perennial. However, because there is no obvious general solution to this problem, I have decided that over the short term, some basic data will be collected at sites that turn out to be dry at the time of the sampling visit. The resulting quantification of the extent of "potential" stream habitat, or of the relative proportion of total stream habitat that is perennial, may turn out to be important over the long term as changing climatic conditions alter local hydrology.

Table 1. List of sites sampled in 2006 with brief physical description.

Site name	Sampling date	Description
Chitina River Tributaries		
Chitina trib W. of Tana	June 17, 2006	Small 1st order stream with extensive canopy
Chakina River	June 18, 2006	Large river delta braided channel - limited canopy
Chitina trib E. of Tebay	June 19, 2006	2nd order high-gradient forested stream
McCarthy Road sites		
Swift Creek	July 15, 2006	2nd order high-gradient forested stream
Nabesna Road sites		
Chalk Creek	June 23, 2006	3rd order low-gradient pool-riffle limited canopy
Rock Creek	July 16, 2006	2nd order low-gradient pool-riffle limited canopy
Chalk Creek Resample	September 22, 2006	
Rock Creek Resample	September 21, 2006	
Jack Creek at bridge	September 21, 2006	Large 4th order low gradient stream with lake source
Skookum Creek	September 22, 2006	Very high-gradient 2nd order alluvial stream
Little Jack Creek	September 23, 2006	3rd order low-gradient forested stream
Fly-in sites in NE part of WRST		
Gravel Creek	August 1, 2006	high-gradient alluvial intermittent stream (flowing)
Beaver Creek	August 2, 2006	deep narrow low-gradient lake outflow in tundra
Rock Lake outflow	August 3, 2006	medium-sized pool riffle lake outflow
Ptarmigan Creek	August 4, 2006	large pool-riffle lake outflow

Of the remaining 28 streams I visited, 15 could not be sampled for other reasons. 4 were at flood stage; unfortunately, these were Chitina River tributaries that could not be revisited later in the year. One other Chitina River tributary was too small and overgrown to be sampled, and yet another could not be sampled because there was no safe landing area for boats. 5 other sites turned out to be wetlands or beaver ponds with little or no flow, 2 were on private land and 2 were too small to sample. In the end, 13 unique stream reaches (22% of sites visited) were successfully sampled (Figure 1, Table 1). Two of these (Chalk Creek and Rock Creek, both along the Nabesna Road), were sampled twice – once in early summer and once in the autumn. In addition, multiple replicate samples of invertebrates and diatoms were collected from the same reach of Chalk Creek during the early summer visit.

Reach definition

Sampling reaches were defined using guidelines from the EPA's EMAP Wadeable Streams Assessment methods (USEPA 2004), and modified as necessary. A sampling reach was defined as 40 times the mean wetted width of the stream, based on 5 equally spaced measurements at the bottom of the proposed reach. Although this length was initially chosen as the minimum sufficient to adequately capture fish community composition in wadeable streams (Reynolds *et al.* 2003), it is also generally long enough to include a complete meander bend, which is a fundamental unit of stream geomorphology. Hence, a reach sufficiently long to encompass a meander bend should adequately capture the habitat complexity of that section of stream (Kaufmann *et al.* 1999). The minimum sampling reach length was set at 150 meters, and the maximum at 500 meters (the latter for feasibility and safety reasons). Reaches were selected to be as representative as possible of the stream section in which they were embedded; in addition, major tributary junctions were avoided and reaches near road crossings were located so as to begin at least 50 meters upstream. Once defined, the reach was subdivided into 10 equally spaced sections by the placement of 11 cross-sectional transects (A – K). These transects formed the framework around which the bulk of biological and physical sampling occurred.

Biological sampling

Macroinvertebrate and diatom sampling was conducted at all 15 site visits. Electrofishing was conducted at a small subset (3) of these and at one additional site along the Chitina River where no other sampling occurred. Riparian vegetation sampling was conducted at 3 sites, and Level 3 Viereck community classification was informally conducted at 5 sites. Biological sampling protocols were largely adopted from the EMAP WSA Field Protocols (USEPA 2004) and from methods developed at the Western Center for Monitoring and Assessment of Freshwater Ecosystems at Utah State University (Hawkins *et al.* 2003).

Macroinvertebrate samples were collected as follows: a modified net that combines elements of Surber and D-net samplers with a 500 μm mesh was used. At each transect, the net was placed in the stream either on either the left, center or right (haphazardly), 1 meter upstream of the first transect. The position of the first placement was determined by rolling a die, and net placements at subsequent transects followed the pattern left-center-right-left…*etc*. An area of 0.09 m^2 in front of the net opening (as defined by a hinged frame that could be lowered to the stream bed) was thoroughly searched for macroinvertebrates by individually rubbing cobbles in front of the net opening and subsequently disturbing the remaining substrate by raking to a depth of approximately 10 cm. A total of 8 macroinvertebrate samples was collected and composited into a single reachwide sample. This sample represents a total of 0.72 m^2 of streambed. Macroinvertebrates and organic detritus were separated from cobble and gravel and preserved in

70% ethanol. Macroinvertebrates were sorted and identified to the lowest practical taxonomic level, generally genus, by Mike Cole, a taxonomist for ABR, Inc.

Benthic diatoms were collected as follows. At each of the 8 transects where macroinvertebrates were collected, an appropriate cobble was haphazardly selected along the same cross section used for macroinvertebrate sampling (1 meter upstream of the transect itself). Cobble selection was shifted one "unit" to the right (*i.e.*, if macroinvertebrates were collected in the center, a cobble was selected on the right). Cobbles were scrubbed and scraped to remove diatoms and material collected was composited into a single reachwide sample. The total volume (diatoms plus rinse water) was recorded and a 40 mL subsample was removed and preserved with 2 mL Lugol's solution. Benthic diatoms were identified to the lowest practical taxonomic level, generally species, by Julia Eichmann, a diatom taxonomist for Ecoanalysts, Inc.

Electrofishing was qualitative and somewhat haphazard, as no protocol had been established. We used a Smith-Root backpack electrofisher powered by a gas generator. All likely habitats were fished, and we generally had 2 netters attempting to collect stunned fish. Due to inexperience on the part of some of the crew, a number of stunned fish were not captured. Wherever possible, these fish were identified and recorded. Captured fish were anesthetized with a mixture of clove oil and ethanol, identified and fork lengths were recorded. Because the riparian vegetation work was very preliminary and exploratory, those data will not be discussed here.

Physical/chemical data collection

We used a HACH Hydrolab sonde to collect temperature, specific conductivity, pH and dissolved oxygen *in situ*. Data were collected in riffles and generally in midstream at the bottom of the reach. *In situ* alkalinity was measured using a HACH field titration kit. In addition, water chemistry samples were collected for later laboratory analysis. The samples included an unfiltered sample for total nitrogen and total phosphorous and a filtered sample for nitrate, ammonium, phosphate and common ions. These samples were frozen at the site using a cooler supplied with dry ice. A third filtered sample, collected for dissolved organic carbon and silicon analysis, was kept at room temperature to prevent the formation of irreversible silicon aggregates.

Physical channel data were collected at 10 of the 13 sites. Physical data collection protocols were largely based on EMAP WSA protocols (USEPA 2004). At each transect, we measured depth (5 measurements), width (wetted and bankfull), channel height (bankfull and incised), undercut banks, canopy cover (6 measurements) and substrate size class (using a gravelometer – 5 measurements at depth locations). In intertransect segments, we measured thalweg depth and habitat type (10 measurements), width (1 measurement), substrate (5 cobbles along width measurement cross-section), woody debris (by size class) and fish cover (macrophytes, filamentous algae, boulders and undercut banks (qualitative estimate of extent). We measured reach slope using a transit level at some sites. We also measured discharge at a subset of sites using a Marsh-McBirney flowmeter and a topsetting wading rod.

Results and Discussion

Physical setting

Despite the small number of streams sampled, we were able to capture reasonable variability in physical and chemical characteristics (Table 2). Due to constraints imposed by safe wadeability, the streams were generally small. I hope in future years to develop safe methods for sampling larger (nonwadeable) streams, as these constitute a large proportion of CAKN streams. Alkalinities were generally low; in contrast, conductivities were fairly high, at least in comparison to pristine streams in the mountain west of the lower 48, with which I am most familiar. Many of the streams drained calcareous geology, which is typified by relatively high loads of dissolved ions.

Table 2. Ranges and means of selected habitat descriptor values for 2006 WRST streams.

Descriptor	Minimum	Mean	Maximum
Elevation (meters)	198	816.7	1342
Wetted width (meters)	1.7	4.3	7.3
Alkalinity (μg/L)	31	92.3	169
Conductivity (mS/cm)	109.9	298	813.2
Total N (μg/L)	150	360	920
Nitrate-N (μg/L)	<1*	160	383
Total P (μg/L)	10	29.5	136
Soluble PO_4-P (μg/L)	<1*	4.3	27
N:P Ratio	2.6	94	411
DOC (mg/L)	0.96	3.3	6.1

*below method detection limit (MDL).

The ratio of nitrogen to phosphorous (N:P ratio) in the water column can be used as a rough guide to nutrient limitations in an aquatic ecosystem. Generally speaking N:P ratio refers to soluble nutrients rather than total nutrients, although this is not always the case. The rule of thumb is that when the N:P ratio is above 16, the ecosystem is phosphorous limited, and when it is below 16, the ecosystem is nitrogen limited. This threshold, known as the Redfield ratio, was developed from studies of marine plankton, but is commonly applied to freshwater ecosystems as well. Most of the WRST streams I sampled had very high N:P ratios (Table 2), suggesting P limitation. The mean N:P ratio of 94 is almost 6 times higher than the Redfield ratio. A notable exception to this pattern is the 3 lake outflows, which had very low N:P ratios (mean = 5.1), suggesting N limitation. This effect of lakes on stream nutrient chemistry has been observed in other systems as well (Arp or Wurtsbaugh ref). However, without knowing the C:N:P ratios in various ecosystem compartments (*e.g.*, periphytic algae or fungi), it is difficult to say anything

9

definitive about nutrient limitations based solely on stream water values, no matter how suggestive (Elser 2004). In general, nitrate-N levels were substantially lower than total N (mean total N:nitrate-N = 2.26), suggesting a substantial load of dissolved organic nitrogen (DON), although DON was not quantified directly. Again, the lake outlet streams were quite different, with much higher total N:nitrate-N ratios observed (mean = 168). Skookum Creek was unusual in that it had high concentrations of both total phosphorous and soluble phosphate (53 µg/L and 27 µg/L, respectively), as well as high levels of total nitrogen and nitrate (500 µg/L and 186 µg/L, respectively).

Macroinvertebrates

Larval macroinvertebrates can typically be identified to the genus level. However, in some cases, species-level identifications can be made with confidence. In other cases, a particular organism may only be identifiable to the family or even order level. This often happens with early instar larvae or damaged specimens. Given that these differences in taxonomic certainty will vary among samples, it is necessary to develop a set of rules regarding which taxa are truly unique if we are to make comparisons among samples. For example, if a sample contains organisms identified variously as *Drunella doddsi, Drunella spp.*, Ephemerellidae, and Ephemeroptera, does it contain 1, 2, 3, 4 or more unique mayfly taxa? In some cases it is possible to make educated guesses. For example if *D. doddsi* is the only *Drunella* species found in the region, then we might assume that organisms identified as *Drunella spp.* are in fact *D. doddsi*. However, in a vast and understudied area like the Central Alaska Network, where the distributions of most taxa are very poorly defined, guessing is probably not a good idea. The solution to the problem is to designate so-called "operational taxonomic units", or OTUs, that define what is and what is not a unique taxon in a given set of samples (or in a region). Depending on the taxon, this may involve "collapsing" some species level identifications to genus, for example. OTUs must often be developed separately for different regions, as taxonomic certainty can also vary depending on various factors (presence or absence of similar taxa, differences in size, etc.). I have begun the process, in collaboration with Mike Cole of ABR, Inc., of developing OTUs that will apply to macroinvertebrate samples from WRST streams. I will also be working with Sandy Milner to investigate whether a common set of OTUs can be developed for DENA and WRST. Ideally, we will be able to use a single set of OTUs for all CAKN streams. In the following discussion, unique taxa are defined by the OTUs we have developed to date. It should be kept in mind that taxonomic richness as defined by OTUs is conservative; that is, the true species or generic richness will always be higher than OTU richness.

A total of 84 unique macroinvertebrate taxa were collected during the 15 site visits. Most of these taxa were genera, although some specimens could only be identified to the family level. 47/84 of the taxa collected (56%) were dipterans (true flies), 5 were trichopterans (caddisflies), 9 were plecopterans (stoneflies), and 11 were ephemeropterans (mayflies). The rest (12) were non-insect taxa, including gastropods and bivalves. The high proportion of dipteran taxa is typical for Alaskan streams, which tend to be dominated by chironomid midges. In these samples, chironomids contributed an average of 5.7 taxa/stream, or 31% of total richness. This is somewhat higher than is generally the case in temperate streams, but substantially lower than is often reported for boreal and arctic streams. Total taxa richness (S) varied widely among the streams, ranging from 4 to 30 unique taxa, with a mean richness of 18.4. When chironomid midge taxa were excluded, richness varied from 2-20 unique taxa, with a mean of 12.4. The lowest richness was found at the intermittent site (Gravel Creek). This is not surprising as only early colonizing taxa would be expected in such a highly disturbed habitat. The highest total richness was at Beaver Creek (S=30), a lake outflow, with the other lake outflows also showing high richness (S = 24, 26). Lake outflows generally have relatively stable hydrology and high productivity, which probably contributes to the increase in macroinvertebrate richness I observed (Table 3).

Densities varied from a low of 14/m^2 (Gravel Creek) to a high of nearly 18,000/m^2 (Rock Lake outflow)(Table 3). The streams with the highest densities were all lake outflows, which again is not surprising given the stable nature and high productivity typical of such streams. These lake outlets were numerically dominated by black flies (*Simulium spp.*), which constituted 33-74% of total individuals collected in these streams. Rock Creek was dominated by a single genus of stoneflies (*Ostracerca spp.*), both in the summer and fall. In contrast, nearby Chalk Creek was dominated by the ubiquitous mayfly *Baetis bicaudatus* in the summer; this taxon was nearly absent from the fall sample, which was dominated by the chironomid genus *Diamesa spp.* This suggests that seasonal variability in community composition can differ substantially among WRST streams, even when those streams are only a short distance apart (less than 10 miles) and are ostensibly similar to one another.

Table 3. Community composition of WRST streams by density. Totals equal more than 100 because Chironomidae are a subset of Diptera. Lepidoptera are butterflies and moths; Ephemeroptera are mayflies; Plecoptera are stoneflies; Trichoptera are caddisflies, Diptera are true flies and Chironomidae are non-biting midges. Total is the total density (#/m^2) of macroinvertebrates in the stream.

	Percent of total density							
Site	Noninsect	Lepidoptera	Ephemeroptera	Plecoptera	Trichoptera	Diptera	Chironomidae	Total
Chitina trib W. of Tana	3.33	0.00	0.00	78.89	0.00	17.78	13.33	125
Chakina River	3.36	0.00	54.20	18.49	0.00	23.95	12.18	331
Chitina trib E. of Tebay	1.06	0.53	71.65	7.22	0.88	18.66	3.80	789
Chalk Creek	3.91	0.00	49.64	26.16	2.85	17.44	6.63	3122
Chalk Creek Resample	9.50	0.00	5.96	28.31	1.49	54.75	37.69	537
Rock Creek	0.37	0.00	19.11	69.94	0.00	10.58	3.92	3208
Rock Creek Resample	0.72	0.00	0.72	88.35	0.00	10.22	4.53	3100
Swift Creek	0.00	0.00	59.61	7.23	2.12	31.04	10.13	1575
Gravel Creek	60.00	0.00	0.00	0.00	0.00	40.00	18.75	14
Beaver Creek	27.68	0.00	0.00	2.14	1.75	68.42	25.04	14250
Rock Lake Outflow	7.43	0.00	0.74	0.00	3.53	88.29	11.98	17933
Ptarmigan Creek	13.31	0.00	0.95	0.95	1.14	83.65	11.11	17533
Jack Creek @ Bridge	19.43	0.00	3.64	13.36	6.07	57.49	35.94	2167
Skookum Creek	30.13	0.00	3.84	4.80	1.73	59.50	42.08	4342
Little Jack Creek	8.99	0.00	3.24	67.99	1.08	18.71	5.95	386

NMDS ordination (not shown) of the invertebrate data (log-transformed to reduce the effects of variations in abundance between samples) showed 3 distinctive groupings. Although it is difficult to reach firm conclusions based on limited data, it appears that the overriding influence on differences in community composition among these samples was seasonal. The exceptions to this pattern were the lake outlet streams, which clustered together, and the intermittent stream, which was an outlier. The observed biological similarity among the lake outlets is consistent with ideas that they may constitute a coherent ecosystem type, at least in some settings (e.g., Robinson and Minshall 1990, Hieber *et al*. 2005). The other two groupings seen in the ordination appear to have little in common aside from the time of sampling (late June/mid-July vs. late September). The samples from the two sites that were revisited group according to season rather than site. These results are somewhat at odds with expectations, and will require further investigation. Interestingly, the community compositions at Rock Creek and at Chalk Creek move similar distances and in the same direction in ordination space from summer to fall.

Replicate sampling

At Chalk Creek during the June site visit, 5 replicate macroinvertebrate samples were collected from the reach. Each sampling effort was offset from the last by one meter (moving upstream) and the starting point was shifted one place to the right. For example, if for the first sample collection started at transect A on the left, collection for the second replicate would start one meter above transect A in the center. Otherwise, each replicate sampling effort was conducted as identically as possible (*i.e.*, the same researcher collected all 5 samples). The objective of this effort is to estimate how accurately a single composite sample captures the species composition and relative abundances that characterize the macroinvertebrate community in the sampling reach. This effort will be continued in coming years as funding allows (collecting replicate macroinvertebrate samples raises the laboratory costs for a site from $750 to nearly $1700). The results of the initial effort were encouraging. NMDS ordination (not shown) demonstrates that the replicate samples were very similar to one another. The mean Bray-Curtis distance (a measure of compositional dissimilarity, and the basis for NMDS) among the replicate samples was only 0.14 (where 0 means samples are identical and 1 means they share no taxa in common), whereas the mean Bray-Curtis distance among all samples was 0.83. In other words, the replicate samples were very much more similar to each other than they were to samples from other streams, or than any other two samples were to each other. Although preliminary, as they are based on a single stream, these results suggest that a single composite sample does a reasonable job of capturing community composition at the reach scale, at least in some streams. Apart from any real differences in species composition and relative abundance among the replicate samples, additional variability is introduced because each replicate was subsampled (a minimum of 500 organisms/sample are typically identified in macroinvertebrate monitoring programs, but the actual number can vary, and in some cases fewer than 500 may be collected). This introduces 2 types of errors, one due to differing numbers of organisms being identified, and one due to compositional differences between the subsample and the entire sample. The latter error can be magnified when the subsample is a relatively small percentage of the total number of organisms in the sample (*e.g.*, Cao *et al*. 2002). In other words, even two identical samples will typically appear to differ to some degree due to the effects of subsampling error. The presence of rare organisms also contributes to variability among subsamples; typically, therefore, rare organisms are excluded from biological assessments that are based on measures of compositional similarity (though there is disagreement over this practice). The effects of rare organisms on similarity can be seen in the Chalk Creek samples, where all of the variation in species arises among very rare (low abundance) organisms, mainly various chironomid midges. Some additional variation in Bray-Curtis distance is generated by modest differences in the abundances of the more common taxa.

Benthic Diatoms

Diatom richness was in general much higher than macroinvertebrate richness, ranging from 7 to 59 species or varieties (mean = 38, median = 41), with a total of 166 unique taxa collected. This suggests that diatom communities might provide more responsive and sensitive indicators of ecological condition in CAKN streams than macroinvertebrate communities, which are much more widely used in streams in the Lower 48. Cell densities varied from a low of $5.8 \times 10^7/cm^2$ (Chitina tributary west of the Tana) to a high of more than $8 \times 10^{10}/cm^2$ (Jack Creek)

The dominant diatom taxon at the Chitina River sites was *Achnanthes minutissima*, which is thought to be characteristic of disturbed habitats (Biggs *et al.* 1998). However, using the model proposed by Biggs *et al.* many diatom taxa are defined as characterizing disturbed habitats. Indeed this same taxon also dominated the communities at Beaver Creek and the Rock Lake outflow, which should be very stable habitats. Furthermore, it was absent from Gravel Creek, which was almost entirely populated by *Meridion circulare*. This is very surprising, as according to Biggs *et al.*, *Meridion circulare* should be most competitive in stable, oligotrophic habitats. Gravel Creek, being subject to intermittent flows, was clearly a highly disturbed habitat, and was also apparently relatively nutrient rich (TN = 340 μg/L, TP = 13 μg/L, TN:TP = 11). However, soluble phosphate was below the detection limit (< 1 μg/L), so much or most of the phosphorous may have been refractory. Chalk Creek was heavily dominated by *Cocconeis placentula var. lineate* in late June. However, this taxon was largely absent from the September sample, which was dominated by *Rhoicosphenia curvata*.

Diatom densities were much higher in September than in the summer. At both Chalk Creek and Rock Creek diatom densities increased by nearly 2 orders of magnitude (40 fold at Chalk Creek, 50 fold at Rock Creek). Such an increase is probably a combination of two factors – the increase in direct sunlight available after leaf fall, and a general increase in biomass throughout the summer in streams that are not regularly scoured by spates. Species richness was also considerably higher in the fall, for reasons that are unclear this early in the project. NMDS ordination (not shown) suggested that, as was the case with macroinvertebrates, seasonal influences on community composition are substantial. The two sites that were resampled showed strong and coincident shifts in community composition, and streams sampled early or late clustered on the ordination accordingly. There were 3 notable exceptions to this pattern. The 3 lake outlet streams clustered together and were extremely similar in terms of species composition (mean Bray-Curtis distance = 0.11, versus an overall intersite mean of 0.66). This is consistent with the patterns seen with both macroinvertebrates and water chemistry and suggests that these ecosystems, although well separated spatially, are fundamentally similar (e.g., Hieber *et al.* 2005, Robinson and Kawecka 2005). Two sites were outliers, located well away from the other sites in ordination space. One of these was Gravel Creek, which is an intermittent system. This stream was completed dominated by a single diatom species, *Meridion circulare*, that constituted nearly 98% of the individuals collected. Although *M. circulare* is not generally considered to be a

13

pioneer or colonizing species, it is clearly acting as such in this system. The other outlier was an unnamed tributary of the Chitina River that was small and heavily shaded, although it is not clear if these characteristics are responsible for the substantial biological difference between this site and the other streams in the data set. This stream was also strongly dominated by a single species, *Achnanthes minutissima* (98% of individuals), in this case one that has been recognized as a colonizing species.

Mats of *Didymosphenia geminata* were noted at 4 sites (the 3 lake outlet streams plus Rock Creek). This species is recognized as invasive in many areas (Spalding and Elwell 2007); it is considered to be native to Alaska, although it is usually found in low abundance. In the past, *D. geminata* was generally considered to be an indicator of oligotrophic or pristine conditions in boreal streams; however, lately there is concern that the species has become invasive within its native range, which is unusual. There is some thought that it may be due to a genetic variant, or a response to anthropogenic alteration of the environment. Given the ability of *D. geminata* to create mats that dominate stream beds nearly completely (Spalding and Elwell 2007), it will be important to monitor the distribution and abundance of this species in CAKN streams.

Two types of replicate sampling were conducted for diatoms. First, 5 replicate samples were collected from the same reach of Chalk Creek, as was done for macroinvertebrates. This replication will allow us to get some idea of how representative each composite sample is of actual diatom biodiversity within the sampling reach, or in other words the sampling error. Secondly, one of these replicates was subsampled 5 times in the laboratory. This replication will allow us to get some idea of how representative the 800-valve subsample is of the actual taxonomic composition of the composite reach sample, or in other words the error associated with subsampling. Variability among the replicate reach samples was substantially higher than was the case for macroinvertebrates, with a mean Bray-Curtis distance of 0.33 (versus 0.14 for replicate macroinvertebrate samples). This may in part reflect the higher taxonomic richness of diatom communities in these streams; mean taxa richness for diatoms was 38 versus 18 for macroinvertebrates. Although Bray-Curtis distance among replicates was still substantially lower than the average distance among all samples (mean = 0.66), the representativeness of the composite reach sample is clearly more of an issue for diatoms than it is for macroinvertebrates. Part of the sampling error is associated with subsampling, as the mean Bray-Curtis distance among laboratory subsamples was 0.1. Interestingly, total taxa richness was more variable among replicate subsamples (ranging from 30-45) than it was among replicate reach samples (40-48, with most samples being in the range of 44-48). Despite these differences, however, the identities of the 2 most dominant taxa were consistent across all 5 replicate reach samples, and the 3rd through the 5th most dominant taxa were generally similar.

Fish
Fish data were collected at a handful of sites using electrofishing. At the first site electrofished, the Chakina River, a total of 24 fish were captured by a crew of 4. Only small braids and backchannels were electrofished and the total time of sampling was less than 45 minutes. 3 species were collected: Dolly Varden, arctic grayling and slimy sculpin. At the second site, the Chitina tributary east of the Tebay River, 9 fish (Dolly Varden and slimy sculpin) were captured. Electrofishing conditions here were less than ideal, as it was a relatively high gradient, high velocity stream. Finally, at Chalk Creek (June sampling visit), no fish were captured despite

14

extensive efforts. The reason for this is not clear, but there may have been a problem with the electrofishing unit itself, as I volunteered to put my hand in the water at the end of the sampling effort and was not rewarded with a noticeable shock. Fish (arctic grayling and slimy sculpin) have been reported in Chalk Creek previously (Markis *et al.* 2004), so we expected to capture them. Although electrofishing was reasonably effective at two of the three sites it was attempted, I intend to use it in combination with other methods (seine netting, minnow traps and angling) next year. One advantage of these other techniques is that they are not subject to Alaska Department of Fish and Game restrictions, and they are much easier to conduct with small crews. In addition these methods may be more effective in situations where electrofishing is difficult and/or ineffective (turbid water, fast water, deep water).

Summary and conclusions

The 2006 field season yielded several important results. At a practical level, significant progress was made toward the development of efficient field data collection protocols for wadeable streams. The protocol as currently envisioned allows a crew of 2 to collect the essential data in 3-5 hours, depending on the size of the stream. In that time were are able to collect water chemistry data and samples, macroinvertebrate and benthic diatom samples, trap and identify fish, collect a variety of physical habitat data, and characterize the reach in terms of riparian condition, fish habitat quality, etc. In 2007, I intend to extend these studies to further improve the data collection protocols for the CAKN flowing waters monitoring program.

Although only a relative handful of streams were sampled in 2006, a number of potentially important conclusions can be drawn based on these preliminary data. First, the majority of streams that appear on blue-line USGS maps are probably not sampleable; this finding will continue to have an important influence on study site selection procedures in the future. Secondly, water chemistry, macroinvertebrate communities and diatom communities are highly variable across the landscape in WRST. This emphasizes the need for a robust classification approach to reduce the influence of spatial variability. Third, diatom richness is substantially higher than macroinvertebrate richness, which is low compared to temperate streams; this suggests that diatom-based metrics may be more sensitive and robust indicators of ecological condition in CAKN streams.

Literature Cited

Biggs, B.J.F., R.J. Stevenson and R.L. Lowe. 1998. A habitat matrix conceptual model for stream periphyton. Archiv für Hydrobiologie 143:21-56.

Cao, Y., D. D. Williams & D. P. Larsen. 2002. Comparison of ecological communities: the problem of sample representativeness. Ecological Monographs 72:41-56.

Hawkins, C., J. Ostermiller, M. Vinson, R.J. Stevenson and J. Olson. 2003. Stream al invertebrate, and environmental sampling associated with biological water quality assessments. Unpublished report, Western Center for Monitoring and Assessment of Freshwater Ecosystems, Utah State University, Logan, Utah.

Hieber, M., C.T. Robinson, U. Uehlinger and J.V. Ward. 2005. A comparison of benthic macroinvertebrate assemblages among different types of alpine streams. Freshwater Biology 50:2087-2100.

Kaufmann, P.R., P. Levine, E.G. Robison, C. Seeliger and D.V. Peck. 1999. Quantifying physical habitat in wadeable streams. EPA/620/R-99/003. U.S. Environmental Protection Agency, Washington, D.C.

Markis, J., E. Veach, M. McCormick and R. Hander. 2004. Freshwater Fish Inventory of Denali National Park and Preserve, Wrangell-St. Elias National Park and Preserve, and Yukon-Charley Rivers National Preserve, Central Alaska Inventory and Monitoring Network. Wrangell St. Elias National Park and Preserve, Copper Center, Alaska.

Reynolds, L., A.T. Herlihy, P.R. Kaufmann, S.V. Gregory and R.M. Hughes. 2003. Electrofishing effort requirements for assessing species richness and biotic integrity in western Oregon streams. North American Journal of Fisheries Management 23:450-461.

Robinson, C.T. and G.W. Minshall. 1990. Longitudinal development of macroinvertebrate communities below oligotrophic lake outlets. Great Basin Naturalist 50:303-311.

Robinson, C.T. and B. Kawecka. 2005. Benthic diatoms of an Alpine stream/lake network in Switzerland. Aquatic Sciences 67:492-506.

Spalding, S. and L. Elwell. 2007. Increase in nuisance blooms and geographic expansion of the freshwater diatom *Didymosphenia geminata*: recommendations for response. Unpublished White Paper.
(http://www.epa.gov/region8/water/didymosphenia/White%20Paper%20Jan%202007.pdf). Accessed May 18, 2009

Sterner, R.W. and J.J Elser. 2002. Ecological Stoichiometry: the Biology of Elements from Molecules to the Biosphere. Princeton University Press, Princeton, New Jersey.

USEPA. 2004. Wadeable streams assessment: field operations manual. EPA841-B-04-004. U.S. Environmental Protection Agency, Office of Water and Office of Research and Development, Washington, D.C.

Whitford, L.A. and G.J. Schumacher. 1968. Notes on the ecology of some species of fresh-water algae. Hydrobiologia 32:225-236.

NPS 100026, May 2009

www.ingramcontent.com/pod-product-compliance
Lightning Source LLC
Chambersburg PA
CBHW080944290526

45795CB00007BA/2887